Vegetarian Wok

COOKBOOK

50 Recipes For the Greens, Tofu And Plant-Based Asian Dishes.

Maya Zein

© **Copyright 2021 by Maya Zein - All rights reserved.**

This document is geared towards providing exact and reliable information in regard to the topic and issue covered. The publication is sold with the idea that the publisher is not required to render accounting, officially permitted, or otherwise, qualified services. If advice is necessary, legal or professional, a practiced individual in the profession should be ordered.

From a Declaration of Principles which was accepted and approved equally by a Committee of the American Bar Association and a Committee of Publishers and Associations.

In no way is it legal to reproduce, duplicate, or transmit any part of this document in either electronic means or in printed format. Recording of this publication is strictly prohibited and any storage of this document is not allowed unless with written permission from the publisher. All rights reserved.

The information provided herein is stated to be truthful and consistent, in that any liability, in terms of inattention or otherwise, by any usage or abuse of any policies, processes, or directions contained within is the solitary and utter responsibility of the recipient reader. Under no circumstances will any legal responsibility or blame be held against the publisher for any reparation, damages, or monetary loss due to the information herein, either directly or indirectly.

Respective authors own all copyrights not held by the publisher.

The information herein is offered for informational purposes solely and is universal as so. The presentation of the information is without contract or any type of guarantee assurance.

The trademarks that are used are without any consent, and the publication of the trademark is without permission or backing by the trademark owner. All trademarks and brands within this book are for clarifying purposes only and are owned by the owners themselves, not affiliated with this document.

Contents

INTRODUCTION 7

CHAPTER 1: TRADITIONAL ASIAN WOK GREENS TOFU BASED RECIPES 11

1.1 Traditional Asian Wok Tofu Scramble 12

1.2 Traditional Asian Wok Udon with Tofu and Greens 14

1.3 Traditional Asian Wok Sesame Pepper Tofu with Greens .. 16

1.4 Traditional Asian Wok Seared Tofu with Beans and Coconut Sauce 18

1.5 Traditional Asian Wok Mixed Greens with Tofu 20

1.6 Traditional Asian Wok Greens with Teriyaki Tofu Dressing 22

1.7 Traditional Asian Tofu Tacos with Chili 24

1.8 Traditional Asian Sofritas Tofu 26

1.9 Traditional Asian Wok Garlic Tofu 28

1.10 Traditional Asian Wok Tofu Noodle Soup 30

1.11 Traditional Asian Wok Banh Mi with Sticky Tofu 32

1.12 Traditional Asian Wok Spicy Tofu Burritos 34

1.13 Traditional Asian Veggie Bowl with Oyster Mushroom 36

1.14 Traditional Asian Wok Ginger Garlic Tofu with Veggie 38

1.15 Traditional Asian Vegan Tofu Bowl 40

CHAPTER 2: TRADITIONAL ASIAN WOK PLANT-BASED RECIPES 43

2.1 Traditional Asian Wok Vegetarian Bibimbap Bowl 43

2.2 Traditional Asian Red Lentils 45

2. 3 Traditional Asian Bo Xao Dau 48

2.4 Traditional Asian Veggie Salad 50

2.5 Traditional Asian Com Chay 52

2.6 Traditional Asian Mi Xao Rau Cai 55

2.7 Traditional Asian Veggie Noodles 57

2.8 Traditional Asian Koora Cabbage 59

2.9 Traditional Asian Chickpea Bowl with Lemon Tahini 61

2.10 Traditional Asian Burrito with Creamy Veggie Sauce 63

2.11 Traditional Asian Yellow lentils with Spinach 65

2.12 Traditional Asian Veggie Rice with Cottage Cheese 67

2.13 Traditional Asian Wok Quinoa Veggie Bowl 69

2.14 Traditional Asian Wok Che Troi Nuoc 71

2.15 Traditional Asian Wok Canh Kho Qua 75

CHAPTER 3: ASIAN WOK VEGAN RECIPES 78

3.1 Asian Spicy Vegan Tofu Enchilada 79

3.2 Asian Vegan Picadillo 81

3.3 Asian Vegan Poke with Watermelon 83

3.4 Asian Vegan Ginger Veggie 85

3.5 Asian Vegan Rice Ball Dessert 87

3.6 Asian Vegan Mung Bean Donuts 90

3.7 Asian Vegan Banana Blossom Salad 94

3.8 Asian Vegan Red Tofu with Curry Sauce 96

3.9 Asian Vegan Banh Gio 98

3.10 Asian Vegan Corn Congee 101

CHAPTER 4: MOST FAMOUS ASIAN VEGETARIAN WOK RECIPES 103

4.1 Asian Vegetarian Wok Spicy Garlic Edamame 104

4.2 Asian Vegetarian Wok Veggie with Peanut Butter Sauce . 106

4.3 Asian Vegetarian Wok Korean Bok Choy 108

4.4 Asian Vegetarian Wok Di San Xian 110

4.5 Asian Vegetarian Wok Teriyaki Cauliflower and Kale 112

4.6 Asian Vegetarian Madras Curry 113

4.7 Asian Vegetarian Spinach and Potatoes with Tofu Kofta 115

4.8 Asian Vegetarian Veggie Butter Curry 117

4.9 Asian Vegetarian Wok Spinach Ravioli 119

4.10 Asian Vegetarian Spicy Pasta 121

CONCLUSION 123

Introduction

The intricacies and explosions of tastes in Asian food are worth checking out. The roots of this cuisine may be traced back to 3000 B.C. when one of the earliest Asian and Indian nations was discovered.

This culinary evolution did not occur on its own. It is, however, due to European colonies moving to the northwest and southwest. Historically, several of the nations were colonized by European forces and were part of the southern area. Vietnam, Laos, and Cambodia, for example, were previously French possessions. Malaysia was a British colony, whereas the Dutch ruled Indonesia. It all improved the traditional southern cuisine and introduced additional elements that are now part of Asian cuisine. It is no mystery that Asian cuisines foods have similar tastes and fundamental materials in their recipes, yet there are still significant variances between them.

Chinese influences heavily inspire Vietnamese cuisine. Basil is a frequent ingredient in Thai cooking, and it originates in Europe. Citrus tastes, on the other hand, are a significant element of Malaysian and Indonesian cuisine. Tofu, greens, and plant-based meat replacements for beef, hog, and chicken have a rich history in the Greater China region—and a tasty future. Plant-based meats have been a part of the broader China culinary landscape for millennia, a practice that dates back to Buddhist monasteries in dynasty China.

Some of the textures and tastes found on the Asian cooking menu are sweet, spicy, and citrus. Ginger, pepper, garlic, and fish sauce are other prominent ingredients in many Asian dishes. Each Asian nation has its signature cuisine with distinct textures and flavors.

The Vegetarian Asian cuisine is most likely heart-healthy. Because of the focus on fruits and vegetables, whole grains, and rice, Asian meals are low in fat, saturated fat, and fiber. They also conform to the medical community's generally recognized concept of a heart-healthy diet, lowering cholesterol and blood pressure while preventing heart disease.

Before you can begin cooking Asian cuisines, you must first become familiar with several main ingredients. If you plan to do some sort of Asian cuisine, soy sauce is perhaps the most important product to have on hand. It is a dark-colored sauce with a thick, salty flavor that is made from soybeans and wheat. It is a common and traditional staple used for coating, fermenting, and cooking in various Asian cuisines, especially stir-fries. Anchovy extract from fish is widely used as a cooking sauce in Southeast Asia to give a spicy, savory flavor to dishes.

Fish sauce has a strong taste, so a little goes a long way. It has a strong odor, so once applied to a dish, it adds a layer of umami, and it is a taste you will know from Thai and Vietnamese cuisine. Stir-fries, soups, and noodle dishes are all good places to start. It should be noted that it is produced from preserved anchovies, so it should not be used for any vegetarian dishes.

The taste of sesame oil is unique, nutty, and herbal. It is used as a sauce or spice, and it is usually applied towards the end of the cooking process to keep the taste. Since it is very potent, it is only used in small quantities. Chili sesame oil is also accessible, and it is a perfect way to get a great sesame taste while also adding some sun. To save it from becoming rancid, keep it in the freezer. Hoisin sauce is a thick and flavorful sauce made from ground soybeans and starch and flavored with red chilies and garlic.

Vinegar, Chinese five-spice, and sugar are popular additions. While the term hoisin comes from the Chinese word for seafood, the sauce does not contain any seafood. Meat, fruits, and noodles profit from the sweetness and saltiness when marinated, stir-fried, dipped, and glazed. It is a popular ingredient in Chinese and Vietnamese cuisine.

Chili peppers, vinegar, cloves, sugar, and salt are used to make Siracha chili sauce, a delicious hot sauce. It is thought to have started in Thailand. The mildly spicy chili garlic sauce may be used for dipping, slicing, marinating, or stir-frying. It has a mildly coarse feel and a nice tang from the vinegar. Oyster sauce is a popular ingredient in Chinese family cooking. It is used as a coating or dipping sauce for meat and vegetables. It is traditionally made from oysters that have been slowly simmered.

We have stereotyped our perceptions of Asian cuisine. Steamed rice, noodles, stir-fried vegetables, and sometimes a side of dumplings, along with the obligatory fortune cookie. This is what we are usually aiming for when we "go Asian" tonight. However, Asian cuisine is more than simply rice, stir-fried vegetables, noodles, and soy sauce. There is a lot more to it than that. Here are some of the most widespread misconceptions regarding Asian meals that should be addressed at the very least.

There are no more diverse cuisines on the planet than those found in Asia. Each nation has its cuisine, which is as diverse as it is numerous. Japan has its unique tastes, Korea has its unique procedures, and Indonesia has its unique spices. You will discover all of these things and more, not just to tempt your taste buds but also to immerse yourself in the culture.

Spices abound over the continent, as do ideas for using them in cooking. Asian food is much more than soy sauce, rice, dim sum, and stir-fries. Healthy steamed foods, Asian-inspired barbecues, a range of noodle soups from various areas, and Asian-style steaks are all available.

We have stereotyped our perceptions of Asian cuisine. Steamed rice, noodles, stir-fried vegetables, and sometimes a side of dumplings, along with the obligatory fortune cookie. This is what we are usually aiming for when we "go Asian" tonight. However, Asian cuisine is more than simply rice, stir-fried vegetables, noodles, and soy sauce. There is a lot more to it than that. Here are some of the most widespread misconceptions regarding Asian meals that should be addressed at the very least.

Rice and noodles are almost usually included in every meal. Asians get their carbs from this source. Steamed eggs, grilled pork, vegetables, deep-fried fish, and various other items, all seasoned with specific spices, might be included.

In certain Asian nations, the dish may even be served without rice or noodles. This clearly proves that Asian cuisine is not only about rice and noodles. Consider these dishes: satay from Malaysia, sushi from Japan, pajeon from Korea, and kebabs from the Middle East.

Foods from Asia are not only Chinese, Japanese, or Korean. This is a complete misunderstanding. These three nations are not the only ones with Asian cuisine. There are additional nations that can provide as many, if not more, Asian culinary options. In this book, you will study the Asian Vegetarian recipes made with the help of Wok. Let's get started.

Chapter 1: Traditional Asian Wok Greens Tofu Based Recipes

Flavorful cuisines are common in Asian countries. They are the start of your day. If you eat healthy and fresh in your day, it is guaranteed that you would feel the same throughout the day. Recipes in this chapter are for vegetarian persons. Let's get start.

1.1 Traditional Asian Wok Tofu Scramble

It is invigorating, tasty, and filling, the kind of food that will keep me satisfied until lunchtime. If you are a vegetarian, I believe you will like this dish since it is quick and simple, rich in protein, and flavorful, which is rare in vegetarian breakfast meals. I hope you will give it a chance even if you are not vegetarian.

This tofu scramble dish is flavorful because of seasonings, yeast, and a touch of mustard. It is a terrific way to switch things up if you are bored with eggs, and it is so delicious that it is worth cooking even if you are not. To prepare this delicious Tofu Scramble, all you need is a block of tofu and four nutritious ingredients. It is a plant-based and healthy egg alternative recipe.

Time taken: 10 minutes

Servings: 2

Ingredients:
- A quarter tablespoon of turmeric
- One block Tofu, drained but not pressed
- One tablespoon of yeast
- Cashew cream, three tablespoons
- Salt and pepper as per your taste
- One cup water

Instructions:

1. Take a wok. Crush up the block of tofu with your hands because the chunks will disintegrate during the cooking time. You can easily split them up with a spoon later if they are too big.
2. Place a wok over a moderate flame on the stove and add all the seasonings.
3. Mix it all and let it cook for five minutes.
4. Add any vegetables of your liking if you are making a scramble.
5. When the mixture starts to boil, pour the water and cream into the wok and bring to boil. Allow 8-10 minutes for the tofu to simmer down, stirring regularly to achieve equal cooking.
6. As it cooks, the water will begin to dry from the wok.
7. Make it thick according to your taste.
8. Remove it from the wok and sprinkle salt and pepper according to your taste. Serve it.

1.2 Traditional Asian Wok Udon with Tofu and Greens

Udon noodles are thick wheat noodles that are popular in Japanese food and are the most often used noodles in brothy soups. They are identical to soba noodles and are ideal for slurping up your tasty soup. It is a fast and simple meal that amazes us despite its simplicity.

It is fantastic all-around since it provides a boost from the leafy greens, a kick from the spice, and stamina from the protein. You may also add chopped vegetables, beans, or peanuts to the mix. Every time you prepare it, you will have a fresh supper thanks to all of the wonderful add-ins and alternatives. The richness and depth of the taste of the broth are crucial to the success of noodle meals like this one. If the broth is flavorful, anything put to it, such as the tofu and noodles, will be flavored as well. The salinity of the soy sauce, the nutty flavors of the sesame oil, and the heat of the red chilies will make this soup enticing and soothing.

If you like noodle dishes as much as we do, this recipe will quickly become a favorite. This recipe is full of protein-rich tofu, nutrient-dense vegetables, filling noodles, and a hearty broth. Let's get started.

Time taken: 35 minutes

Servings: 2

Ingredients:

- Fifteen ounces of Udon noodles
- Seven teaspoons of peanut oil
- Sesame oil
- Vegetable oil
- Fifteen ounces of slices of firm tofu
- Salt and pepper as per your taste

- Ten ounces of Asian greens, any type
- One bunch of onions, thinly sliced
- One teaspoon of red pepper
- A third of a cup of soy sauce
- One teaspoon of sugar

Instructions:

1. Boil the noodles according to the package directions.
2. Drain and set aside approximately 1/3 cup of the cooking liquid.
3. In a wok, heat two tablespoons of oil over medium heat.
4. Season the tofu all over with salt and pepper after patting it dry.
5. Sear the tofu in the pan for approximately 2 minutes on each side, or until golden brown. Remove from the oven and keep warm.
6. Toss the greens and one tablespoon of oil into the skillet.
7. Cook, occasionally stirring, until the spinach is barely wilted.
8. Combine the remaining ingredients together in a mixing bowl.
9. Add it in wok. Bring it to a boil to make a broth.
10. Toss the noodles and greens together in dishes.
11. Serve it with the tofu.

1.3 Traditional Asian Wok Sesame Pepper Tofu with Greens

This salad with sesame-coated tofu is a game-changer. This sesame tofu is simple to prepare and full of flavor, making it ideal for a filling vegetarian breakfast. Before being pan-fried till crispy, the tofu is marinated. You may bake it, but I found that frying the tofu yielded the best results for me.

Time taken: 55 minutes

Servings: 3

Ingredients:
- Two tablespoons oil
- Two hundred grams sliced tofu, fried
- A quarter teaspoon of asafetida
- Two red chilies, sliced
- One piece of sliced fresh ginger
- Two tablespoons black beans
- A quarter cup of corn four
- One tablespoon of soy sauce
- Two tablespoon of wine
- Two cups of boiling water or any quantity you required
- Half teaspoon sesame oil
- One teaspoon sesame seeds, toasted

- Green pepper, one
- Salt and pepper as per your taste

Instructions:

1. Heat the vegetable oil in a wok.
2. Insert the asafetida into the heated oil and cook for 20 seconds before adding the other ingredients. Stir it well.
3. Add all other ingredients in it.
4. Cook for two minutes, stirring regularly, in the pan with the sliced tofu.
5. Mix in the seasonings and spices.
6. Stir in hot water once everything is properly blended.
7. Cook for two to three minutes, or until the sauce has thickened.
8. Drizzle in the sesame oil and top with sesame seeds before serving.

1.4 Traditional Asian Wok Seared Tofu with Beans and Coconut Sauce

The tofu was formerly thought to be a food eaten only by Asians or hippy vegetarians. It is, nevertheless, becoming even more prevalent nowadays. You may also grill the tofu and use it in a variety of meals. You must cook or sear it with a sprinkling of oil, salt, and pepper for the searing purpose. It is more flavorful and nutritious than deep-fried tofu, while it is not as filling. The pan-seared tofu may also be eaten straight from the fridge. The first frying on a dry pan effectively removes surface moisture from the tofu, eliminating the need to blot or drain it beforehand. The seared tofu is cooked with green beans and a coconut sauce in this dish.

Time taken: 55 minutes

Servings: 4

Ingredients:
- One package firm tofu
- Two tablespoon of soy sauce
- A quarter cup of vegetable oil
- One tablespoon garlic, coarsely diced
- One tablespoon fresh ginger, peeled and chopped
- Half spicy red pepper flakes (dry)
- One pound green beans
- One red bell pepper, thinly sliced
- Salt and pepper as per your taste

- One can unsweetened coconut milk
- One tablespoon lime zest
- Half cup of salted roasted cashews, chopped
- Rice noodles or rice

Instructions:

1. Chop the tofu first.
2. Place chopped tofu in a dish. Pour soy sauce over it. Let it marinate for ten minutes.
3. Heat the oil in a wok over medium heat until it is hot but not scorching, then add the tofu in one layer and cook until it turned brown or for approximately 5 minutes total.
4. Transfer to a large dish with a spoon, retaining the oil in the pan.
5. Add the spices and minced garlic to the wok and let it cook until it turns fragrant.
6. Add the beans, bell pepper and minced ginger. Cook while stirring constantly.
7. Bring the coconut milk and remaining tablespoon of soy sauce to a boil, reduce to low heat, cook for six minutes or until the beans are soft.
8. Using a spoon, transfer the veggies to the platter with the tofu.
9. Cook until the sauce has thickened slightly and been reduced to about 3/4 cup, approximately 2 minutes.

10. Pour the sauce over the veggies and tofu after adding the lime juice.

11. Cashews should be sprinkled on top.

1.5 Traditional Asian Wok Mixed Greens with Tofu

This dish is a take on Saag Paneer. Making healthier renditions of classic Indian meals is one of my favorite pastimes. When I am strapped for time and want to pack a tasty punch with some leafy greens, this cuisine is one of my go-to meals. Saag is a Punjabi term that means "leaf-based" or "greens." That means any mix of greens may be used in this dish: spinach, mustard greens, kale, and the choices are unlimited.

Time taken: 35 minutes

Servings: Eight

Ingredients:
- One medium bag of mixed greens
- One medium onion
- One medium garlic clove
- Two Tomatoes, chopped
- Twelve almonds, soaked in water for ten minutes
- One block firm tofu, cut into cubes
- Half teaspoon turmeric powder

- Half teaspoon cumin powder
- Two pods cardamom
- Cinnamon stick
- Half teaspoon cumin seeds
- Four green chilies
- Salt and pepper as per your taste
- Oil

Instructions:

1. Coarsely cut the mixed greens and simmer for 5 minutes in boiling water until wilted.
2. Heat the oil in a wok and sauté the garlic and onion until it turns transparent.
3. Let it cook for a few minutes with the cardamom, clove, cinnamon, and green chilies.
4. Add the chopped tomatoes and continue to simmer until the tomatoes are soft.
5. Reheat the wok and gently sauté the Tofu pieces until they are lightly browned on both sides. Set aside for now.
6. Add the cumin seeds to the pot and reheat with some oil.
7. Cook for 5 minutes after adding the spices and the tofu.
8. Serve with parathas when still hot.

1.6 Traditional Asian Wok Greens with Teriyaki Tofu Dressing

Teriyaki Asian noodles with tofu and stir-fried veggies are as good as take-out. This teriyaki tofu is a quick and tasty weekday meal. The crispy fried tofu in a sweet and salty prepared teriyaki sauce will be a hit. This is a simple and fast dish. It creates a high-protein breakfast for busy days when served over brown rice.

Time taken: 35 minutes

Servings: 2

Ingredients:
- 555g Baby bok choy
- Choy sum, 450g
- 450g beans
- One cup of vegetable oil
- One finely sliced onion
- 60 g soft brown sugar
- Half teaspoon chili powder
- Two tbsp. fresh ginger, grated
- Teriyaki sauce, 255 mL
- One tbsp. sesame seed oil
- 600g firm tofu, firm and drained

Instructions:

1. Baby bok choy and choy sum should be cut into thirds widthwise.
2. Heat a wok to a high temperature. Swirl in 1 spoonful of the oil to coat the side. Stir-fry the onion for 3-5 minutes, or until crisp, over medium-high heat. Using a slotted spoon, remove the chicken and drain it on paper towels.
3. Heat another tablespoon of oil in a wok.
4. Stir-fry the greens in batches for 2-3 minutes, or until barely done, using more oil if necessary. Remove from the heat and keep warm.
5. Combine the sugar, chili, ginger, and teriyaki sauce in a mixing bowl, pour it into the wok, and boil for three minutes.
6. Simmer for 2 minutes with the sesame oil and tofu, rotating once until the tofu has broken up.
7. Top the greens with the tofu mixture and fried onion, then serve.

1.7 Traditional Asian Tofu Tacos with Chili

The advantages of a plant-based diet are undeniable. Plants are good for both the health and the environment. Increasing the number of them can only help you in the long term. Most people frequently dislike tofu. On the other hand, tofu is high in protein, inexpensive, and absorbs the taste of anything you put on it.

Freezer-friendly and full of flavor. If you are not already a lover of tofu, Tofu Tacos could just convert you. For those strapped for time on weeknights, easy to meal prep and have on hand for tacos or bowls. This dish is suitable for vegetarians.

Time taken: 55 minutes

Servings: 5

Ingredients:
- Sixteen ounces of tofu (pressed and dried)
- A quarter cup of soy sauce
- One tablespoon of lemon zest
- Vegan mayonnaise
- Salt, pepper, and chilies as per your taste
- One cup of cabbage and avocado (chopped)
- Seven tortillas
- Half cup of scallions

Instructions:
1. Cut tofu into 1-inch cubes.
2. Sprinkle lime zest and soy sauce over the tofu and place it aside.
3. Fry the chopped vegetables in a wok over moderate flame.
4. Meanwhile, coat tofu with corn starch and mix it in the above pan. Cook it until it turns brown, and vegetables turn tender.
5. Reheat the tortillas on the skillet or wok.
6. Assemble the cooked mixture along with sauce over the tortillas.
7. Serve it with any topping.

1.8 Traditional Asian Sofritas Tofu

This vegan version of Sofritas Tofu tastes even better than the actual. It is peppery, crunchy, hearty, and satisfying, and it's great in tacos, burritos, or by itself. Make your own Tofu Sofritas at home instead of going to a restaurant. This simple vegan filling is ideal for classic bowls, burritos, and tacos.

Time taken: 60 minutes

Servings: 8

Ingredients:

- One block of tofu (dried properly and cut into cubes)
- Olive oil
- One cup of each red and green pepper (diced)
- One cup of onion (diced)
- Salt, pepper, chili, and cumin as per your taste
- One tablespoon of tomato puree
- One cup of tomatoes (roasted and chopped)
- Half cup of broth (vegetable)

Instructions:

1. Firstly, preheat the oven up to 220C. Grease a baking dish.
2. Place cubes of tofu in the baking dish and sprinkle oil over it. Bake it for 10 minutes or more. Then, set it aside.
3. For the preparation of sofritas, sauté all the vegetables and spices in a deep pan.
4. Add baked tofu, broth, and spices (if you want to) in the above deep pan. Put a lid on it and boil it for 15 minutes over low flame.
5. Thicken the consistency of the mixture as per your liking.
6. Add lime zest over it and serve in a dish.

Note: you can also make this recipe in a wok.

1.9 Traditional Asian Wok Garlic Tofu

It is a crispy Asian Garlic Tofu recipe that has a savory, salty, and sweet taste. For a truly wonderful vegetarian supper, you can serve it with broccoli and rice. For a truly wonderful vegetarian supper, serve with broccoli and rice. This spicy garlic tofu comes together quickly and easily, requiring just 10 minutes to prepare. It is deliciously served over rice with stir-fried veggies on the side.

It is a spin-off of the classic Sichuan dish Mapo tofu. However, in this version, garlic is the star, and it is also a little milder. In addition to the spicy bean sauce, we use sweet hoisin sauce and skip the Sichuan peppercorns. It is also less difficult to create.

Time taken: 35 minutes

Servings: 2

Ingredients:
- One box of tofu that is extra firm
- A quarter cup of hoisin sauce
- One tablespoon of sugar
- One teaspoon ginger
- Two garlic cloves, minced
- A quarter teaspoon of red pepper flakes
- One tablespoon oil
- One tablespoon of sesame seed oil

- Salt, chili and pepper

Instructions:

1. Remove the tofu from the package. Cover the tofu with extra paper towels and place it on top of the platter. Place a hefty object on top, such as a cast-iron pan. Allow for 30 minutes of resting time.
2. Combine Hoisin sauce, soy sauce, sugar, ginger, garlic, and red pepper flakes in a medium mixing bowl.
3. Tofu should be cut into bite-sized pieces. Toss in a bowl with the sauce to coat. Allow for 30 minutes of resting time.
4. Heat the olive oil over a moderate flame in a wok.
5. When the wok is very hot, add the tofu. Flip once the underside is properly seared. Continue to cook until the bottom is charred.
6. Remove from heat and drizzle with sesame oil.
7. Serve with anything.

1.10 Traditional Asian Wok Tofu Noodle Soup

The classic chicken noodle soup gets a simple and tasty makeover. It is a Thai-inspired dish. It has a chicken soup flavor. However, it is made with tofu. This dish is designed exclusively for vegan soup fans.

Time taken: 35 minutes
Servings: Four

Ingredients:
- One tbsp. rapeseed oil
- One tablespoon ginger root, minced
- Two minced garlic cloves
- Salt and pepper as per your taste
- Half pound fresh mushrooms, sliced
- One cup reduced-sodium chicken broth
- One cup chicken broth with low sodium
- A quarter cup soy sauce
- Seven oz. tofu, rinsed, cubed and firm
- One cup snow peas
- One big shredded carrot
- Two finely sliced green onions
- Eight oz. Chinese egg noodles
- Finely chopped peanuts

Instructions:

1. Heat the oil in a wok over a moderate flame.
2. Add the ginger, garlic, and pepper flakes. Heat and stir for 1 minute or until fragrant.
3. Bring to a boil the mushrooms, stock, sherry, and soy sauce.
4. Cook for 5 minutes, uncovered.
5. Add all the spices and chopped vegetables in it.
6. Reduce heat to low and continue to cook, uncovered, for another 4-6 minutes or until veggies are crisp-tender.
7. Meanwhile, prepare the noodles as directed on the box.
8. Drain and divide into four bowls.
9. The soup should be poured over the noodles.
10. Sprinkle with any garnishing.

1.11 Traditional Asian Wok Banh Mi with Sticky Tofu

When I am in a picky mood and cannot decide what to eat, I always go toward Asian food. It is always something I can make in a short period of time.

These sticky tofu banh mi bowls are a quick and simple recipe that can be ready in 15 minutes. The textures and tastes in this Tofu Bánh M are well balanced. It is seasoned in sesame oil, tamari, and Sriracha sauce to give the extra firm tofu spicy, delicious umami taste. These bowls are a variation of the typical Vietnamese banh mi sandwich, which is made with vegetables.

Time taken: 35 minutes

Servings: 2

Ingredients:
- One packet of tofu
- One tablespoon of avocado oil
- One tablespoon of soy sauce
- Two tablespoons of Hoisin Sauce
- One tablespoon of Sriracha
- Half cup of rice noodles
- One cup of lettuce shredded
- Half cup carrots, thinly sliced or shredded
- Half cup of cucumbers sliced thinly
- Half cup red cabbage shredded, or

red cabbage selected
- One handful of chopped cilantro
- One avocado, in slices
- Seeds of sesame for topping

Instructions:

1. Let's start with our sticky tofu being packed.
2. Chop the tofu into cubes and put on medium-high heat in a hot pan with the oil.
3. Enable about 3-5 minutes to tan and then flip the cubes on either side to brown.
4. Turn off the heat and toss the soy sauce, hoisin sauce, and Sriracha until each side is golden brown and crispy.
5. Cook the rice noodles according to the instructions in the box.
6. Serve it with veggies and noodles.

1.12 Traditional Asian Wok Spicy Tofu Burritos

Tofu comes in soft, firm, and extra-firm variants. They are easy to prepare, readily adaptable to fit your preferences, and perfect for quick evening dinners. These sofritas in the recipe provide a lot of flavor to the dish overall.

Time taken: 55 minutes

Servings: 2

Ingredients:
- Two cups of lime rice
- One cup of black beans
- One avocado
- Red pepper
- One cup of Spicy tahini dressing

For Tofu:
- One block extra firm tofu
- One tablespoon of olive oil
- Two teaspoons of coconut sugar
- Three teaspoons of corn
- Paprika, salt, and pepper
- Two teaspoons of garlic
- One teaspoon of onion powder
- A quarter teaspoon chili powder

Instructions:

1. Heat two spoons oil in a wok.
2. Take the tofu and extract the excess moisture from it.
3. Stir fry tofu in a wok. Add all spices and sugar in it. Mix it well.
4. Add sriracha mixture in it.
5. When it turns light brown, remove it from heat.
6. Assemble all prepared things and ingredients over tortillas.
7. Serve it with any sauce.

1.13 Traditional Asian Veggie Bowl with Oyster Mushroom

This Asian-inspired vegetable bowl is simple to prepare and great to eat. It is inherently vegan, but because of the meaty oyster mushrooms, you would never guess. Mushrooms are also beneficial to your health. It boosts the immune system, protects the brain from oxidative stress, and helps prevent breast cancer. Mushrooms may improve your health if you eat them regularly. Let us get started with this recipe.

Time taken: 35 minutes

Servings: 2

Ingredients:
- Two tiny turnips or one daikon
- Half cup of vinegar
- One tablespoon of sugar
- Salt and pepper as per your choice
- For Mushrooms oyster:
- 250 g of mushrooms and oysters
- One tablespoon of tamari
- One tablespoon of Sriracha
- Half teaspoon of sugar
- 1 teaspoon of vinegar
- Half teaspoon of sesame oil
- Other ingredients:

- 1 cup brown and cooked rice
- 1 cup of broccoli (chopped)
- Half cucumber (finely sliced)
- Small cabbage (thinly sliced)
- Half avocado (finely chopped)
- Peanuts (optional)

Instructions:

1. Clean the daikon and peel it. Cut it into very thin strips.

2. In a small pot, add vinegar, ½ cup of water, sugar, salt, and chili flakes, and bring it to a gentle boil. After 10 minutes, remove it from the flame.

3. In the above pot, put the sliced daikon. Put the lid on it and stick it in the fridge for at least one day before use. Let it cool.

4. Mix all the ingredients of mushroom oyster together in a pan.

5. Let it marinate for a while. Set it aside.

6. Heat up a frying pan on moderate-high heat after the mushrooms have been pickled for 15 mins or so.

7. With a little bit of oil, clean its surface and put the mushrooms on it once the pan is heated.

8. Grill the mushrooms until they are golden-brown and cooked through. Make sure you keep an eye on them all the way, so they do not roast.

9. Assemble all the ingredients in your bowl as per your liking and serve it with a dressing and a sauce.

1.14 Traditional Asian Wok Ginger Garlic Tofu with Veggie

This ginger garlic vegetarian tofu stir-fry with brown rice is loaded with bell peppers, broccoli, and snow peas, and it makes terrific leftovers that you can enjoy cold from the fridge. When I want something tasty but healthy without cheese or bread, I turn to these ginger garlic tofu vegetable bowls. It is easy to get into a take-out rut as a vegetarian, particularly if you often do not cook or meal-prep.

These Asian-style ginger garlic tofu vegetable bowls are far from ordinary. They provide a well-balanced meal that includes vegetables, protein, carbohydrates, healthy fats, vitamins, and minerals. It becomes practically easy after a few attempts.

Time taken: 55 minutes

Servings: 2

Ingredients:
- For the Sauce:
    - Two teaspoons of tamari
    - Two teaspoons of coconut water
    - One teaspoon of ginger paste
    - One teaspoon of lime juice
    - Two garlic cloves
- Veggie Bowl Ingredients:
    - One and half cup of veggie broth

- One cup of rice
- One cup of chopped cilantro
- One small purple cabbage
- 450 g of Brussel sprouts
- One pepper chili
- Tofu
- One tablespoon oil
- Half teaspoon of curry powder
- Half teaspoon of paprika
- Half teaspoon of turmeric powder

Instructions:

1. In your blender cup, put all the sauce ingredients and blend it for 1-2 minutes or until a creamy consistency is achieved by the sauce.
2. In a wok, add the veggie stock and carry it to a moderate boil.
3. Add salt and clean rice to it. Cover it with a lid and let it boil for 15 minutes.
4. Remove from the heat, and once ready to serve, keep the rice under steam.
5. Preheat the oven and prepare a broad-rimmed flat baking tray during the rice preparation.
6. Sprinkle the spices over finely sliced purple cabbage, Brussels, and tofu. Roast them in the oven for 8-10 minutes.
7. Assemble all the ingredients in serving bowls.
8. Serve them with a sauce.

1.15 Traditional Asian Vegan Tofu Bowl

It is a dish in which plates are filled with a zesty coconut lime rice, pieces of sticky and charred baked tofu, and toasted roasted broccoli. Then, with a generous sprinkle of peanut sauce, it is even better. All of the gooey, toasted, zesty fresh flavors and textures are there.

This tofu-based vegan poke bowl is fast, simple, and addictive. Poke is often cooked with tuna or fish, but we will be using diced organic tofu, which absorbs the sesame-ginger seasoning and has a soft texture. It is nutritious, full, and delicious. Tofu poke bowls are a quick and nutritious lunch, supper, or make-ahead dish that can be made in about 50 minutes.

Time taken: 55 minutes

Servings: 2

Ingredients:

- Four cups of farro cooked
- One cucumber, sliced into quarters and chopped
- One cup of tomatoes with raspberry, halved
- One cup of spinach
- One block of extra-firm tofu
- One cup of water

- One tablespoon of vinegar
- One tablespoon of olive oil
- Salt and pepper as per your taste
- Half tablespoon of garlic

For Dressing:

- Half cup of tahini
- Three tablespoons of lemon juice
- Three teaspoons of olive oil
- One tablespoon of soy sauce
- Two cloves of garlic, minced
- Salt and black pepper as per your taste

Instructions:

1. Slice the tofu into eight slices of the same kind. Place the sliced tofu between a folded kitchen-paper and place a heavy flat-bottomed item on top to extract excess moisture. Let the tofu drain until it is touch-dry.
2. Split into cubes with the tofu.
3. Mix the water, the vinegar, the olive brine, the olive oil, the food yeast, the spice, the basil, the garlic powder, and the pepper together. Add the cubes of tofu to ensure sure they are immersed, then marinate overnight.

4. In a mixer, combine the ingredients for the dressing. Blend on strong. When required, taste and change the seasoning.
5. Assemble your bowl as per your choice.
6. Drizzle with any sauce and serve it.

Chapter 2: Traditional Asian Wok Plant-Based Recipes

In this chapter, you will study fifteen different, flavorful and tasty Asian Wok Plant Based recipes. Let's get into it.

2.1 Traditional Asian Wok Vegetarian Bibimbap Bowl

This is a famous Korean recipe. In this recipe, fried tofu is being used. You do not have to be a vegetarian to enjoy this dish, which is topped with seasoned veggies, a runny fried egg, and delicious gochujang sauce. Bibimbap is a traditional Korean meal. The dish is not especially tough or tough, but each component needs a few minutes of prep time to make it ready for the table. The most time-consuming part is chopping and chopping the components.

Time taken: 35 minutes

Servings: 2

Ingredients:
- Four teaspoons of sesame oil
- One cup of carrots (finely sliced)
- One cup of zucchini
- Half cup of Bean sprouts (soaked)
- One mushroom (washed and diced)
- Salt and pepper as per your taste

- Two cups of cooked rice
- Half cup green onions (finely diced)
- Two tablespoons of soy sauce
- A quarter teaspoon of black pepper
- One spoonful of butter
- Three Eggs
- Three spoonfuls of red chili sauce (optional)

Instructions:

1. Warm the oil over a moderate flame in a wok and start cooking the carrot and zucchini in the hot oil for around 3-4 minutes.
2. Mix the bean sprouts, carrots, and mushrooms in it. Let it cook for about 5 minutes and season it with salt and pepper. Set aside the vegetables.
3. Add cooked rice, green onions, soy sauce, and spices in the same wok. Let it simmer for 2 minutes.
4. Melt the butter in a separate wok over moderate heat and gently fry the eggs in it, rotating once until the yolks are still somewhat runny, but the egg whites are solid.
5. Assemble your serving bowl or dish with a hot cooked rice mixture and cover it with a mixture of vegetables and a fried egg.
6. Serve with the sweet red chili sauce.

2.2 Traditional Asian Red Lentils

Lentils are a kind of legume that may be eaten. It is a lens-shaped annual plant with lens-shaped seeds. It grows to be around 40 cm tall, and the seeds are produced in pods with two seeds in each. Red lentils are comparable to the lentils we are all familiar with. The distinction is in color, which is a deep crimson, and the taste, which is more delicate. Iron, fiber, selenium, zinc, carbs, protein, and vitamin B1 are all abundant in red lentils.

In addition, they are high in phosphorus, manganese, and folic acid. Low in fat, these lentils offer just 360 calories per 100 grams. They aid in the prevention of anemia during pregnancy. Many women require iron supplements. We recommend that you continue to take your vitamins while also included these lentils in your diet. Because they are high in starch, they aid in digestion and help to calm despite requiring a large meal. They are easier to digest than regular lentils since they do not have skin.

Furthermore, patients with intestinal and stomach disorders, sluggish digestion, and excess gas will benefit greatly from their ingestion. Red lentils provide essential carbs, vitamins, proteins, and minerals to correct the nerves and brain. As a result, if you have recently had memory issues or other types of issues with your intellectual function, consuming this dish is a good idea. Furthermore, red lentils' health advantages are beneficial to developing children, students, and adults who are under a lot of pressure and worry.

Red lentils have the benefit that they cook in the least period of time, making them ideal for dal curries, winter soups, and thick vegan pasta sauces.

Time taken: 55 minutes

Servings: 1

Ingredients:
- One tablespoon of oil
- One cup sliced onion
- Two (delicately sliced) garlic cloves
- One tablespoon (coarsely diced) ginger
- Four cups of water
- One cup rinsed dried red lentils
- One tablespoon cumin
- One tablespoon of coriander
- One tablespoon of turmeric
- A quarter teaspoon cardamom
- A quarter teaspoon of cinnamon
- A quarter teaspoon pepper
- Salt as per your liking
- Two tablespoons of a paste of tomato

Instructions:

1. Warm the oil over a moderate flame in a medium-sized wok.

2. Add the onion, garlic, and ginger to it.

3. Cook and keep stirring regularly for around 6 minutes.

4. Add water, lentils, vegetables, and salt. Keep stirring continuously.

5. Carry the soup to a low boil, then switch the heat down to low.

6. Cover and cook for around 20 minutes or until the lentils become very soft.

7. Add the tomato paste when well blended. Cook for many more minutes.

8. Serve it and enjoy.

2. 3 Traditional Asian Bo Xao Dau

It is a noodle salad with beans, but it is more of a light meal in Southeast Asia than a starter course and as a salad is generally defined in the West. It includes everything required for a well-balanced meal. It contains carbohydrates, as well as a variety of vegetables and fresh herbs. In this recipe, we will change its ingredients beef or chicken with tofu.

Time taken: 35 minutes

Servings: 2

Ingredients:
- One garlic clove (minced)
- Black pepper and salt as per your taste
- One tablespoon of cornstarch
- Four tablespoons of vegetable oil
- One pack of Tofu, drained and firm
- Half thinly sliced onion
- Two cups washed and cut new green beans
- A quarter cup broth
- Two tablespoons of soy sauce

Instructions:

1. Combine garlic, black pepper, cornstarch, and one teaspoon of vegetable oil in a big mixing cup.
2. Take a wok and heat oil in it.
3. Put tofu in it and let it heat for three to five minutes over a high flame in a broad wok.
4. Place the tofu in a large mixing bowl and put it aside.
5. In a wok, heat the remaining one tablespoon of oil.
6. Cook, constantly stirring, until the onion is soft.
7. Add the green beans and the broth and mix well. Reduce the heat to mild and cover. Simmer for 4–5 minutes, or until beans are crisp and tender.
8. Combine the tofu and soy sauce in a mixing bowl.
9. Cook for 1 to 2 minutes, stirring continuously, or until completely heated.
10. Serve it in a dish by mixing it together.

2.4 Traditional Asian Veggie Salad

This recipe is a really easy one, although it does take a bit of time to prepare. You can add any green vegetable of your liking in this recipe, but I added cabbage, carrots, and green onions, and these are enhanced by a punch of tart lime juice, spicy fish sauce, peanuts, and fresh mint in this veggie salad recipe.

Time taken: 35 minutes

Servings: 2

Ingredients:
- Two cups of green cabbage (chopped)
- Three scallions (chopped)
- Two medium carrots
- Three tablespoons lime juice
- Two tablespoons fish sauce
- One tablespoon white sugar
- One tablespoon rice wine vinegar
- Three tablespoons peanuts (chopped)
- A quarter cup of mint leaves (chopped)

Instructions:

1. If you add any other vegetable in it, you have to sauté it in a wok.
2. You have to chop all the vegetables that you have collected.
3. Place the shredded cabbage in a strainer with a bowl inside it and season generously with salt (the salt will be washed away inevitably, so do not think about going overboard). The salt can assist in wilting the cabbage and removing some of the bitter taste.
4. Allow the cabbage to soften and wilt for a few minutes. Rinse the cabbage vigorously in cool water until it has wilted.
5. Using the cheesecloth, wring out the cabbage in tiny batches to extract as much water as practicable in a big mixing cup, set aside the dried cabbage.
6. Place the carrots in a bowl and julienne them. Pour in half of the white vinegar and sugar, making sure the carrots are fully submerged.
7. Cut the onion as thinly as practicable and blend with the remaining white vinegar and sugar in a mixing dish.
8. If you run out of white vinegar, you can still use some or a little cool water to cover the vegetables.
9. After leaving the carrots and onions to stay for around 10-15 minutes, drain them. The vinegar can be saved for the salad dressing.
10. Combine the carrots and onions with the cabbage and any other vegetable in a large mixing bowl.

11. To begin, pour about two tablespoons of the reserved vinegar into the salad. Combine the starch, salt, and black pepper in a mixing bowl.

12. Mix well and season to taste for more seasoning.

2.5 Traditional Asian Com Chay

Com Chay is also known as burned rice. It is a basic and natural meal that is delicious and appealing. Steamed rice is cut into flat circular shapes to make Cm Chay. Slices of fried rice are fried in a hot oil pan till they become golden and crunchy after drying. Steamed rice, mushrooms, tomatoes, carrots, and seasonings are served with the main ingredient. We would not be using any meat in this dish, but you may substitute tofu or another green veggie.

Time taken: 55 minutes

Servings: 2

Ingredients:
- 250g of glutinous rice
- 250g of ordinary rice
- Cooking oil
- Scallion
- Spices (chili powder, Fish sauce, salt, and pepper)

Instructions:

1. Soak the glutinous rice for 1-2 hours before serving, then combine it with regular rice and wash.
2. Place in the rice cooker and cook according to the package directions.
3. Note: To render the rice a little drier than normal, apply one tablespoon of cooking oil and a pinch of seasoning powder.
4. Place the cooked rice in a tray when it is still high. You will use a wet ladle or a clean cup to press the rice into an even layer on the plate. It should be between 0.3 and 0.4 cm high.
5. Return the rice to its original place, ensuring that all sides are evenly dry. When there is no sunlight, such as in the winter, you may do this process with an oven.
6. Preheat the oven to 110 degrees Fahrenheit and bake for 2-3 hours. You should even place the rice tray in the refrigerator to dry it.
7. Prepare the fish sauce with honey. Pair the fish sauce with the purified water in the following proportions: 3:3.
8. Stir in one tablespoon of chili powder after completely dissolving the water. Cook the scallion in a pan.
9. To drain the scallion, brush it and chop it. Heat oil in a wok over medium flame.
10. Add the scallions to the hot oil and mix rapidly until they are dark green and aromatic. Then, quickly switch off the stove and dump it into a tub.

11. Split the rice into medium-sized portions until it has been dehydrated. Prepare the rice for frying. Turn on the heat and add oil to the wok.

12. Reduce the heat after the oil has heated for a bit.

13. Pour the rice in and fried it on both ends. To minimize cooking oil, take them out and place them on a plate with oil-absorbing cooking paper.

Note: While frying the rice, hold the heat on a low setting. The rice will burn if the temperature is kept too high. Otherwise, feeding at a low temperature would be difficult. Sprinkle one sheet of sugar sauce and one layer of fried scallion on top of the rice after the competition.

2.6 Traditional Asian Mi Xao Rau Cai

Fried veggies is another name for this meal. Stir-fried veggies may be used in a variety of Southeast Asian dishes. They are a tasty addition to grilled or fried meats and shellfish. They may be prepared in a variety of ways, and the combinations of veggies are almost endless. The lack of strong sauces like oyster sauce differentiates the Vietnamese rau xao from the others.

When you add fish to the veggies, the recipe becomes a full dinner when served with rice–easy to make and ideal for those days when work gets in the way. If you are a vegetarian, leave off the fish sauce and replace the beef with tofu.

Time taken: 55 minutes

Servings: 2

Ingredients:
- Two cups of egg noodles
- Half cup of broccoli
- Half cup of peas
- Half cup of carrot (chopped)
- Half cup of celery
- Half cup of bok choy
- Half cup of cabbage (chopped)
- Salt and pepper as per your taste
- Two teaspoons of sugar

- Two tablespoons of soy sauce
- Three garlic cloves
- One onion (chopped)
- Three tablespoons of fish sauce
- Two teaspoons of vegetable oil
- Cilantro (for garnishing but optional)

Instructions:

1. Broccoli, carrots, and celery should be steamed first.
2. Bring water to a boil, then add the noodles and cook for a few seconds before draining.
3. Rinse the noodles in cool water for a couple of seconds before removing them fully.
4. Begin to stir-frying onions and garlic in vegetable oil in a wok over high heat. Sauté all of the vegetables on the high sun.
5. Combine the salt and sugar in a mixing bowl. Continue to cook with the noodles. Toss in the soy sauce.
6. Add as much fish sauce as you need.
7. Use the best judgment to determine if the dish is ready; however, be cautious since the cooking will lead the food to burn.
8. Garnish it with anything.

2.7 Traditional Asian Veggie Noodles

These light and refreshing Asian veggies with noodles, different vegetables, and bean sprouts can be served as a tangy side dish with grilled meats and poultry or as a main dish on its own. You can also eat this as a snack on your own.

Time taken: 65 minutes
Servings: 5

Ingredients:
- Twelve ounces of noodles
- Two carrots (chopped)
- Two cucumbers (chopped)
- Four green onion (chopped)
- Two cups of cups fresh bean
- Half cup cilantro
- Half cup fish sauce
- Half cup rice vinegar
- Two tablespoons sugar
- Two cloves garlic
- Lime
- Salt and pepper as per your taste

Instructions:

1. In a big mixing cup, soften the vermicelli noodles by coating them with boiling water and soaking them for 3-4 minutes.
2. Drain and rinse under cold water before adding to a big mixing cup.
3. Toss the noodles with the diced vegetables, bean sprouts, and minced cilantro.
4. Combine the fish sauce, rice vinegar, cinnamon, garlic, and crushed red pepper in a glass container or a cup.
5. Toss the noodles in 3/4 of the dressing to coat them.
6. If needed, add more dressing. If needed, top with more cilantro and green onion, as well as a squeeze of lime.
7. Salad can be prepared ahead of time and stored in the refrigerator overnight.
8. Serve it as you like.

2.8 Traditional Asian Koora Cabbage

Brassica vegetables like cabbage, spinach, and broccoli are known for their high nutritional value. Cruciferous veggies are an excellent place to start if you are seeking to enhance your diet. Cabbage may guard against rays, prevent cancer, and lower the risk of heart disease. Cabbage leaves may be smooth or crinkled, and the color ranges from green to red and purple.

In this recipe, you will learn how to make tasty Asian Cabbage with Asian spices.

Time taken: 2 hours

Servings: Three persons

Ingredients:
- Cooking oil: 3 tablespoons
- Two chili peppers dried hot, cut into bits
- One tablespoon black split skinned lentils
- One tablespoon Bengal gram flour
- One teaspoon of mustard seeds
- A few curry leaves
- One pinch of powder Asafetida
- Four peppers of green chili, chopped.
- One cabbage head, thinly sliced
- A quarter cup of frozen peas

Instructions:

1. Heat the oil over a moderate-high flame in a wok.
2. Cook the red chili peppers, all types of gram mentioned above, and mustard in the hot oil. If the gram starts browning, add the curry leaves and asafetida powder. Stir it well.
3. Add the green chili peppers and proceed to cook for another 3 minutes.
4. Add the cabbage, peas, and lentils to the combination. Season it with salt.
5. Continue cooking until it starts to wilt but stays a little crunchy for about 10 minutes.
6. Put the coconut into the combination, and simmer for another 2 minutes.
7. Instantaneously serve and enjoy.

2.9 Traditional Asian Chickpea Bowl with Lemon Tahini

This dish is perfect for a weekday supper or whenever you need a fast, nutritious meal made with basic ingredients. It is great to have a couple of meals like this for those lazy evenings when you do not feel like cooking but need to use up some vegetables and yet want to eat something nutritious.

This vegan chickpea dish is filling, filling, and flavorful. It is packed with healthy vegetables, including broccoli, zucchini, bell pepper, fresh basil, almonds, and lemon tahini sauce, and takes just twenty minutes to prepare.

Time taken: twenty minutes

Servings: 2

Ingredients:

For the chickpeas:
- One cup of Chickpea (rinsed and drained)
- Two teaspoons of Olive oil
- Half tablespoon of cumin field
- Half teaspoon of crushed garlic
- Half teaspoon of paprika smoked
- Half teaspoon of kosher salt
- Half teaspoon of turmeric teaspoon

For the dressing of the lemon tahini:
- Half cup of tahini
- One minced garlic clove

- One tablespoon lime juice
- A quarter cup of hot water
- Salt and pepper as per your taste

For the bowls:
- 1 cup of quinoa rice (cooked)
- 1 cup of lettuce (chopped)
- 1 cup of tomatoes (chopped into halves)
- 1 cup of seedless cucumber (chopped)
- A quarter cup of red onion (sliced)
- A quarter parsley (chopped)
- Half cup of shredded cheese

Instructions:

1. Preheat the oven to 400 ° F.
2. Combine the chickpeas, olive oil, cumin, garlic powder, smoked paprika, and salt in a medium-sized dish. Stir until you have well-coated chickpeas. Put the chickpeas on a broad baking sheet and roast for 30 minutes or until they are crispy.
3. Prepare the lemon tahini dressing when the chickpeas are roasting. Whisk the tahini, ginger, lemon juice, and water together in a tiny bowl or glass. Season it with salt and pepper. Add a little water and whisk again if the dressing is too thick.
4. Put the quinoa, corn, or cauliflower rice into the bottom of a cup to assemble the bowls. Garnish with sliced vegetables.

5. Drizzle with a seasoning of lemon tahini.
6. Serve it with any sauce of your liking.

Note: you can also prepare this in your wok.

2.10 Traditional Asian Burrito with Creamy Veggie Sauce

This easy Vegan Burrito Bowl is very delicious, healthy, and easy to prepare. You will adore it. Warm, fragrant rice and beans are topped with fresh crisp veggies and sprinkled with the most delectable and surprisingly creamy Lime Sauce. It is both vegan and low in fat that will have you wiping the dish.

The Creamy Vegan Cilantro Sauce, prepared with silken tofu, cilantro, jalapeño, and lime juice, is a great addition to your culinary arsenal because once you know how to make it, you can use it as a base for a variety of delicious flavors and dishes.

Time taken: 35 minutes

Servings: 5

Ingredients:
- One cup of brown rice
- One and half cup of black beans (cooked)
- Salt, cumin, chili powder, and yellow pepper (as per your taste)
- Half tablespoon of garlic powder
- One diced tomato

- Half cucumber (finely sliced)
- For Creamy Sauce:
- One package of tofu
- One tablespoon of cilantro
- One garlic clove
- Two tablespoons of lime juice
- Salt and chili as per your taste

Instructions:

1. Add water, rice, salt, and cooked beans in a wok and put it over moderate flame. Cover it with a lid. Boil for about 45 minutes or until the rice are cooked and the water evaporates.
2. Prepare vegetables when rice is cooking.
3. In a food processor, put all the sauce ingredients in it and blend it well or until it turns very smooth.
4. Assemble your bowl or dish. Put lettuce as a base in a bowl, cover it with bean rice mix, and top it with vegetables.
5. Drizzle it with a cilantro sauce and serve.

2.11 Traditional Asian Yellow lentils with Spinach

It is a delectable combination of Bengal gram and green gram, cooked with chopped spinach and traditional Indian spices. This is a dish that I adapted from an Indian dish. It may not seem to be much, but it is extremely delicious. Serve with heated rice or chopped baked potatoes for supper. For a complete dinner, serve with carrots, cabbage, or a fresh sliced tomato.

Time taken: Two hours and thirty minutes

Servings: 5

Ingredients:

- Two cups of yellow split peas (approximately 14 ounces)
- Eight cups of water
- Freshly squeezed lemon juice for two teaspoons (from around one medium lemon)
- Salt two teaspoons, plus more as required
- Eight teaspoons butter unsalted
- Two teaspoons of cumin seeds
- One and half teaspoon of turmeric
- Five big, peeled, and finely minced garlic cloves
- A quarter cup of fresh ginger peeled and finely chopped
- One medium chili serrano stemmed and

thinly chopped
- Spinach, eight ounces, washed and coarsely chopped

Instructions:

1. In a fine-mesh strainer, position the split peas and rinse them vigorously under cold water. Switch to a wide saucepan, add the water you have weighed, and bring to a boil over high heat.
2. Reduce the heat to medium-low and simmer, occasionally stirring and skimming any scum off the surface with a large spoon until the peas are completely soft and the consistency of split pea soup thickens for about 30 minutes.
3. Set aside, remove from the heat, and add the lemon juice and the measured salt in it.
4. Heat the butter over medium heat in a frying pan until it is foamed. Add the cumin seeds and turmeric in it and simmer until the cumin seeds are toasted and fragrant and the butter is very foamy, stirring periodically, for around 3 minutes.
5. Add the garlic, ginger, and serrano; season with salt; and simmer for around 2 to 3 minutes, stirring periodically, until the vegetables have softened. Add the Spinach in it and simmer until the spinach is fully wilted, stirring periodically, for around 4 minutes.
6. With the split peas, move the spinach mixture to the reserved saucepan and mix to blend. Serve with steamed rice or naan.

2.12 Traditional Asian Veggie Rice with Cottage Cheese

This recipe is inspired by a classic Indian dish. It is just a tweaked version of it. This comfort food staple is prepared entirely from scratch and is packed with vegetables. It is a fantastic method to repurpose leftover chilled and processed veggies like onion, carrots, peas, and broccoli. It may be served as a side dish or as a meatless main course.

Time taken: Two hours

Servings: Three persons

Ingredients:

- One cup of Rice Basmati
- One and half of Paneer cubes
- Half cup of Peas & carrot
- One large Onion
- Two Green Chilies
- One teaspoon Ginger Garlic Paste
- Leaves of coriander, diced-as desired
- Salt-As required
- Oil or Ghee

Instructions:

1. For about 30 mins, rinse and soak the rice. On moderate flame, put ghee in a saucepan and let it heat for 3 minutes. Add soaked rice well-drained in it and cook for a while until it becomes dry.
2. Add oil in a wok over moderate flame. Add onion, green chili, and fry until the onion is only translucent, without altering its hue.
3. Add the paste of ginger and garlic, fried it, and then add the vegetables. Fry them to half-finished vegetables.
4. Add 1 cup water and salt in it and let it cook. Add the rice which is already cooked. Cover with a lid, and cook in moderate flame.
5. Prepare the paneer cubes. For better taste, let the paneer cubes be small. Paneer cubes (previously thawed or immersed in hot water) are typically toasted in a nonstick skillet until it turns out to be golden.
6. Once the pulao is accomplished, the paneer is drained and added to the pulao. Before adding, ensure the water is depleted from the cottage cheese.

2.13 Traditional Asian Wok Quinoa Veggie Bowl

It is a simple, plant-based dinner to celebrate spring's abundance. You will feel healthy and pleased after eating this Quinoa Veggie Bowl. A generous spoonful of pesto adds a burst of vibrant, fresh flavor. Nutritious, satisfying, delectable, and appealing. Quinoa Veggie Bowl blends plant protein, fresh spring veggies, bright aromatic pesto, and sliced almonds for crunch.

Time taken: 35 minutes

Servings: 2

Ingredients:
- Three tablespoons of olive oil
- Three carrots (peeled and roughly chopped)
- 15 Brussels (sliced)
- One sliced onion
- One and half cup of peeled acorn squash
- Two beets washed and sliced into wide chunks
- Salt and pepper as per your taste
- One cup of quinoa (uncooked)

- For Dressing:
  - Two tablespoons of vinegar

- Two teaspoons of olive oil
- One spoonful of water
- Two tablespoons of honey syrup
- One tablespoon of mustard
- Salt and pepper as per your taste

Ingredients:

1. Set the oven to 180 Celsius and cover the pan with two baking papers.
2. Slice all the veggies, then place the squash and beets on one pan and place the carrots, Brussels sprouts, and onion on the other pan.
3. Sprinkle olive oil, salt, and pepper over all the veggies.
4. Put the veggies in the oven and bake for 20 minutes. The pan with carrots and Brussels will be ready to come out first.
5. While the veggies are roasting, put a moderate-sized saucepan to a boil with 1 ½ cups of water.
6. Add some salt and quinoa to the boiling water. Cover it with a lid and reduce the heat to low, and let it boil for 15 minutes.
7. Mix all the ingredients of dressing in a separate jar for the maple dressing.
8. Divide the quinoa into serving bowls and cover them with as many roasted veggies as you wish.

9. Sprinkle the maple dressing over serving bowls and serve.

2.14 Traditional Asian Wok Che Troi Nuoc

Rice balls are stuffed with mung bean paste and dipped in a sweet and aromatic ginger syrup. This delicious dessert is both satisfying and reassuring. It is a warm, sticky delicacy that is one of my favorite sweet treats—the somewhat chewy, sticky dough pairs well with the greasy bean interior and oh-so-sweet ginger syrup. For me, this decadently sweet dish harkens back to my youth.

The rice balls' skin is made of rice flour and has a soft, chewy feel. The filling is a mildly sweet, creamy mung bean paste. On chilly autumn or winter days, the combination of rice balls and ginger syrup is sheer bliss. To add a nutty taste and boost the taste of Che Troi nuoc, we normally scatter sesame seeds or chopped peanuts on top.

Time taken: One hour

Servings: four persons

Ingredients:
- One third cup split mung bean, peeled
- Salt and pepper as per your taste
- One cup of water
- Three tablespoons sugar

- One inch fresh ginger
- Three quarts liquid
- One pound of brown sugar

For the Sauce:
- Four tablespoons of water
- One tablespoon of tapioca starch
- Six ounce coconut milk can
- One teaspoon of sugar
- Salt as per your requirement

Instructions:

1. Soak the mung beans overnight after rinsing them many times with water.
2. Combine the glutinous rice flour and water in a large mixing basin and knead until a soft dough forms.
3. Add 1 tbsp. water at a time if the dough is not sticking together. The dough should be wet and pliable, similar to bread dough.
4. For 2-3 minutes, knead the dough. Wrap in plastic wrap and set aside on the counter while you finish the remainder of the steps.
5. Mung beans should be rinsed and drained. Place the beans, along with the salt, in a rice cooker.
6. Pour the beans into the bottom of the cooker and spread them out evenly. Pour in the water. Close the lid and let it cook.

7. Open the cover once the cooker finishes.
8. Mash the beans with a paddle spoon until the individual beans are no longer visible. The beans should resemble mashed potatoes in appearance. Mix in the sugar well. Allow cooling for 10 minutes after transferring the mashed beans to a platter.
9. Take one teaspoon of mashed mung bean and roll it into a ball between your hands. Continue forming balls until you've used up all of the mung beans.
10. Peel and slice the ginger into 1/4-inch thick coins.
11. Combine the water and brown sugar in a medium saucepan over medium heat.
12. Add the ginger slices just as the syrup is about to boil.
13. Cover the saucepan, reduce the heat to low, and set the rear burner to simmer the ginger syrup.
14. In the middle of the dough, place a mung beanball. Work the dough gently around the beanball. Squeeze gently between your hands to form a ball.
15. To make the ball spherical, roll it between your hands.
16. Carry on with these steps to make the rest of the balls.
17. Transfer them to the pot with the ginger syrup using a slotted spoon. Continue rolling and cooking the balls until they are all done. Make tiny dough balls with any extra dough.
18. Cook for another 10 minutes in the ginger syrup once all of the balls have been done.

19. To make a sauce, combine the remaining ingredients in a small saucepan over medium heat. To blend, stir everything together. Add the sauce when the coconut milk just begins to boil, and stir vigorously for 2-3 minutes.

20. Remove the sauce from the heat after it has thickened.

21. To serve, put a few sticky rice balls and some ginger syrup into a dessert dish.

2.15 Traditional Asian Wok Canh Kho Qua

Bitter melon, a pumpkin family member, is cultivated across the tropics in both the West and East hemispheres. Bitter melon is a popular edible vegetable in many countries.

Canh Kho Qua translates to "bitter melon" in Vietnam. Bitter melon is known as Ku gua in Mandarin Chinese. As the bitter melon stews in the fragrant soup, it becomes very delicate and mushy. It is an innate flavor that most people become used to over time and may eventually desire.

Apart from their cultural importance, bitter melons are well-known for their high nutritional content, which has been linked to a variety of health benefits, including diabetes, malaria, and even HIV therapy. Bitter melon extracts are utilized in a variety of products, including tea and supplements.

Time taken: 55 minutes

Servings: Four persons

Ingredients:
- Two melons
- Six cups water
- One finely sliced green onion
- Cilantro sprigs, finely chopped
- One shallot, peeled

- Salt

Veggies:

- Vegetables as per your liking
- One teaspoon of fish sauce
- Salt and pepper as per your taste
- One teaspoon of sugar
- One shallot, chopped
- Half cup noodles, water soaked, any type
- A quarter cup mushrooms, water soaked

Instructions:

1. Combine the vegetables, sauces, spices and all other ingredients in a mixing dish and stir thoroughly. Set aside.
2. Blanching is a method that may be used to decrease some bitterness. Blanch the bitter melon in boiling water for approximately 1 minute, or until it becomes dark green. Remove from the oven and set aside to cool. When the melons are cold enough to handle, cut them crosswise into 1 to 1.5-inch slices.
3. Drive a tablespoon or knife through the green outer flesh and the white pith in the middle. Slowly core out the pith and seeds with a circular motion while holding the bitter melon in one hand and a spoon/knife in the other.

4. Bring the water/stock to a boil with the peeled shallot. Fill the bitter melons with the vegetable fillings.

5. When the water/stock is boiling, add the filled bitter melons and simmer for approximately 15 minutes.

6. Transfer to a soup bowl and top with cilantro and chopped green onion. Serve it.

Chapter 3: Asian Wok Vegan Recipes

Veganism is surprisingly simple to achieve in Asian cuisines. Vegan meals may be found in various sorts of cuisine, from Chinese to Korean delicacies, and are generally focused on plant-based basics like rice, noodles, tofu, or vegetables. So whether you are making a noodle bowl, a stir-fry, or a pot of hot and sour soup, these ten vegan dishes will please you with their Asian-inspired tastes.

Veganism is a sort of vegetarian diet that eliminates all animal-derived foods, including meat, eggs, dairy products, and other animal-derived foods. Many vegans avoid refined white sugar and some wines since they are made with animal ingredients. Vegan is a term that may refer to either a person who follows this diet or the diet itself. For example, the term vegan may be used to describe a culinary item, such as "This curry is vegan."

Although there is some disagreement over whether some items, such as honey, fit into a vegan diet, it is preferable to add on the side of caution and avoid certain items if you are cooking for other vegans or ask your guests. All cereals, beans, lentils, vegetables, fruits, and the practically endless variety of meals formed by mixing them are included in a vegan diet. Fermented foods are common in vegan diets as well. Tempeh, a bean paste product that also exists in a sprouted variant, is a complete food that may be used in lieu of tofu. Other fermented foods like miso and kimchi are also acceptable and promoted in vegan diets. Vegans consume many of the same popular and recognizable daily meals as everyone else, such as green salads, spaghetti, etc.

3.1 Asian Spicy Vegan Tofu Enchilada

I think you should give this dish a try, whether or not you adopt a vegan diet. These Vegan Enchiladas are delicious, nutritious, and will give your dinner routine a nice twist. This dish will take you by surprise in a good way.

Time taken: 40 minutes

Servings: 5-6

Ingredients:
- Six light taco shells or tortillas
- One pack of tofu (dried and cut into cubes)
- Olive oil
- Two teaspoons of seasoning of taco
- Diced tomatoes
- One cup of black beans (rinsed and soaked)
- One diced onion

Instructions:

1. Firstly, preheat the oven up to 220C.
2. Dry out tofu completely. Cut into cubes.

3. Sprinkle seasoning over tofu. Place it in a skillet with oil over moderate flame and cook until it turns brown.

4. Mix the peas, black beans, and onion in a bowl and put aside meanwhile the tofu is frying.

5. Mix together the sauce and chipotle seasoning in a different bowl and set aside. Take half a cup of the sauce and dump it into a greased baking dish to scatter the sauce out over the dish.

6. To prepare the enchiladas: dump into one tortilla a tablespoon of the tomato mixture and then place a fried tofu tablespoon. Fold the tortilla and bring the part of the fold down into the baking dish. Repeat this step until all the enchiladas are completed.

7. Add the remaining mixture sauce over the enchiladas and let it bake for 17 minutes.

8. Serve it.

3.2 Asian Vegan Picadillo

Vegan Picadillo is prepared with tempeh, lentils, and potatoes, is a plant-based variation of this classic Cuban dish. It is filled with bold flavors from Spanish olives, capers, raisins, and spices in a robust tomato foundation. Serve over rice, cauliflower rice, or a bed of zoodles. This dish is delicious.

Time taken: 55 minutes

Servings: Four persons

Ingredients:
- Two cups of broccoli soup
- One cup white rice
- Salt, pepper, and chilies as per your taste
- A quarter cup of cilantro (finely chopped)
- One tablespoon of lemon zest
- Olive oil

For the main:
- One onion (sliced)
- Red pepper bell (chopped)
- One tablespoon of Garlic
- Salt and pepper as per your taste
- One teaspoon of oregano
- One teaspoon cumin

- Two teaspoons of paprika
- Two tablespoons of tomato paste
- Half cup broth of vegetables

For citrus slaw:

- Two avocados (thinly sliced)
- Two cups of cabbage (finely shredded)
- A quarter cup of red onion (cut thinly)
- A quarter cup of olive oil
- One teaspoon of lime zest
- Salt and pepper as per your taste
- For garnish, cilantro, and lime wedges

Instructions:

1. Make rice by using the first six ingredients.
2. Boil broth in a wok or a pan.
3. Add rice and spices in it.
4. Reduce stove temperature and let it cook for fifteen minutes or until all broth has been dried.
5. Add the coriander in it and stir it gently. Rice is prepared.
6. Take a wok and heat oil in it.
7. Add spices and all other ingredients of the second section mentioned above.
8. Saute it properly.
9. Add broth in it. Cover it with a lid.

10. Let it boil over low heat.
11. Prepare the avocado citrus slaw by adding all its ingredients in a mixing dish.
12. Serve all prepared dishes in a plate.
13. Garnish it as you like.

3.3 Asian Vegan Poke with Watermelon

Try this watermelon "tuna" vegan poke dish with sriracha mayonnaise. It is extremely tasty, fresh, and nutritious. You are going to adore it. Poke bowls are a traditional Native Hawaiian dish. Rice, uncooked and cut veggies, and raw fish or tofu make up this nutritious and light dish. It may be served either as a snack or a main meal.

Time taken: 55 minutes

Servings: Four persons

Ingredients:

For the marination:
- Four cups of cubed watermelon
- Two spoonfuls of soy sauce
- Two spoonfuls of sesame seeds
- Five teaspoons of vinegar

For the bowl:
- One cup of brown rice boiled
- One carrot, chopped
- One cucumber, finely sliced

- Two spoonfuls vinegar
- Salt, red pepper
- One cup of seaweed salad
- One cup of finely chopped red cabbage
- One sliced avocado

Instructions:

1. Cut down the watermelon into bite-size cubes.
2. Mix the marinade components in a dish. Over the watermelon cubes, pour the seasoning and gently mix until well mixed. Toss sesame seeds and green onions into them.
3. Move it all into a zip lock bag and put it in the refrigerator. Enable it to marinate for at least overnight.
4. Cut the other items all up. By chopping it into thin slices, begin with the cucumber. Then, mix two teaspoons of rice vinegar, salt, and chili flakes in a small cup. For around 10 minutes, spill it over the cucumber and let it rest.
5. In the meanwhile, cook the remaining ingredients.
6. Mix the vegan mayonnaise with the sriracha sauce. Serve all of it over rice in a bowl.

3.4 Asian Vegan Ginger Veggie

Within 30 minutes, you may have this delicious bowl of food on the table. Sesame tofu stir fry with a sticky, gingery flavor. Serve with rice or grains. The sauce is basic and sweetened with maple syrup. Tofu is crisped, vegetables are roasted, sauce components are added, thickened, and the dish is finished. This was served with brown rice. To make tofu-free, add other vegetables or chickpeas instead of tofu. Bean sprouts or cucumbers may be used to provide crunch. In the winter, serve hot, and in the summer, serve warm.

Time taken: 55 minutes

Servings: Four persons

Ingredients:
- One third cup liquid
- Rice vinegar, half cup
- A quarter cup of soy sauce
- Half teaspoon red pepper powder
- Five garlic cloves
- One teaspoon powdered ginger
- Tamarind paste, one tsp
- Xantham gum, half teaspoon

Instructions:

1. In a blender, add all of the ingredients and mix until smooth. Taste for spiciness and add more red pepper as needed. If the dressing is too thick, then add water at a time until the correct consistency is achieved.
2. Pour over the noodles or greens and toss to combine.
3. To make a stir-fry sauce, put 1 cup of dressing in a wok or nonstick pan, then add veggies and tofu cubes and simmer for 5-7 minutes over medium heat. As required, add more dressing.
4. Keep leftovers in a glass container in the refrigerator for up to 7 days.
5. When ready to dine, split into single-serving containers and pour over noodles or greens.

3.5 Asian Vegan Rice Ball Dessert

Rice ball is also known as Bua Loy. It is a traditional Thai dessert composed almost entirely of rice flour. As we shall see, this dish may be made in a number of forms and colors. These rice balls are made of rice flour, mung beans and other ingredients mentioned below. This dessert recipe is purely vegan.

Time taken: 55 minutes

Servings: Four persons

Ingredients:

For Filling:

- Ten oz. mung beans (peeled)
- Half cup sugar
- Half cup water (warm)
- Half cup coconut (shredded)

For Dough:

- Two cup water or more
- One cup sugar
- One cup rice flour
- Two teaspoons of baking powder
- Half cup of mashed potato flakes

Instructions:

1. Soak mung beans in warm water for at least 1 hour or overnight. Steam for about 20 minutes.
2. Meanwhile, dissolve the sugar in a bowl of warm water. Shift the cooled mung bean to a mixing bowl and coarsely mash it.
3. Mix in the sugar water mixture and the coconut thoroughly. The consistency should be similar to mashed potatoes. Allow cooling before forming tiny quarter-size mung beanballs.
4. Stir together the sugar mixture and the potato flakes in a big mixing bowl to dissolve. Add baking powder until it is fully dissolved.
5. Combine the two forms of rice flour and stir to create a dough disk. The dough would not need to be kneaded. The dough should have the strength of wet playdough.
6. Take off a slice of dough the size of a golf ball and roll it into a ball. Through the palms of your hands, flatten the dough into a disk and thin out the sides to create a pancake.
7. Add a couple of teaspoons of 1/4 cup of water to the dough at a time, combining thoroughly after each addition.
8. Place the filling in the middle and fold the dough edges together, sealing the seams with your palms.
9. Toss in a bowl of sesame seeds until fully covered.
10. Enable to rest for at least 1 hour, wrapped loosely at room temperature.
11. Fry it in a wok filled with hot oil.

12. It is fine to fry many at once unless you want them to be fully immersed in oil for even cooking.
13. Remove and serve.

3.6 Asian Vegan Mung Bean Donuts

Mung beans are a versatile ingredient that may be utilized in both sweet and savory recipes. In Southeast Asia, mung bean paste is a popular filler for sweet desserts. This gluten-free Vietnamese Doughnuts recipe produces incredibly crispy donuts with a sweet sugar frosting. This is a must-try dish for anybody who likes delicious fried sweets. The texture of the doughnuts is really distinctive. They are crispy on the surface and soft and chewy on the inside, comparable to crusty bread but sweeter. The delicious mung bean filling fills half of the donuts, while the remainder is doughnut rings.

Time taken: 55 minutes

Servings: Four persons

Ingredients:

For Filling:

- Half cup of mung bean
- Salt as per your need (most appropriately ¼ teaspoon)
- Half of cup water
- Two tablespoons of sugar
- One teaspoon of vanilla essence
- One tablespoon of vegetable oil

For Dough:

- One small potato

- Half cup of water
- Half cup of boiled water (warm)
- Three tablespoons of sugar
- One cup of rice flour
- One teaspoon of baking powder
- One tablespoon of vegetable oil
- Five cups oil for frying

For glaze:

- One cup sugar
- One teaspoon of vanilla essence
- Two tablespoons of water
- Half tablespoon of lemon juice
- One third cup of sesame seeds (roasted)

Instructions:

1. Fill a wide bowl halfway with cold water and apply the mung beans. Wash and rinse the beans in water. Cover the bowl halfway with cool water, and soak the beans for at least two hours.
2. Fill a rice cooker halfway with beans. Combine the salt and water in a mixing dish. Create an equal layer of beans by spacing them out. Cook on a simple white rice setting with the lid closed.
3. Place the cooked beans in a medium mixing dish.

4. Combine the cocoa, vanilla sugar, and vegetable oil in a mixing cup. Mash the beans with a paddle spoon when they are still sweet.

5. Move tiny filling mounds onto a plate with a medium cookie scoop for a total of 10 mounds.

6. Shape a rough ball by rolling the filling mounds between your hands.

7. Peel and cut potatoes. In a small saucepan, position the potatoes. Add half cup of water. Cook until the potatoes are tender, covered over medium heat. Using a spatula or a spoon, crush the potatoes.

8. In a measuring cup, mix 1 cup boiling water and sugar. Combine the glutinous rice starch, rice flour, and baking powder in the tub of a stand mixer.

9. Combine 1/3 cup mashed potatoes and the vegetable oil in a mixing bowl. Gradually transfer the water and sugar mixture to the mixer on low speed before a dough shapes. Allow for 30 minutes of resting time after covering the dough.

10. Shape donut according to your liking. You also have to fill it with mung beans filling.

11. Cover the donut with a moist towel and put it on a wide tray.

12. Using a medium cookie scoop to scoop tiny mounds of dough onto a tray with the remaining dough. Make a 5-inch long rope out of each mound. Make a loop by joining the ends together.

13. Heat the vegetable oil in a big wok. Heat the oil over low heat.

14. Move the donut rings into the oil with caution. Flip the donuts over until they float to the tip.

15. Place the donuts on a plate that has been lined with paper towels. Remove some extra oil using blotting paper.
16. Make a glaze by combining all ingredients and let it boil over medium heat. Switch the heat off. Allow the syrup to sit for a couple of minutes or until it has darkened in color.
17. Dip the donuts in the glaze, covering one rim, if desired. While the glaze is still sweet, sprinkle roasted sesame seeds on top of the donuts.

3.7 Asian Vegan Banana Blossom Salad

This Thai-inspired banana flower salad has just the right amount of sweetness, spice, sourness, and saltiness. The plating of the banana flower salad is particularly stunning. One of the most unusual and perplexing items I have ever across is a banana flower. So, let's get this started.

Time taken: 55 minutes

Servings: Four persons

Ingredients:
- One banana blossom
- 500 ml ice water
- One tablespoon of lime juice
- Half mango or papaya (chopped)
- One onion (sliced)
- One carrot (sliced)
- Half green pepper (thinly chopped)
- Two teaspoons of coriander
- Two teaspoons of mint
- Four teaspoons of peanuts (crushed)
- Two teaspoons of shallots (fried)

For Marinade:
- Two teaspoons of water

- Two teaspoons of maple syrup
- Two teaspoons of soya sauce
- Two teaspoons of lime juice
- One teaspoon of Garlic
- One teaspoon of shallots
- Chili and salt as per your taste

Instructions:

1. Place the banana blossom layers on top of one another and roll them tightly together.
2. Slice them quite thinly and soak them for 20 minutes in ice water with lime.
3. To make the marinade, combine all of the ingredients in a small mixing bowl and whisk until fully dissolved.
4. In a big mixing cup, toss the banana blossoms, papaya, cabbage, carrot, green pepper, coriander, marinade, and peanuts until well combined.
5. Organize the salad on a serving platter (or, like we did, on a thick piece of banana or cabbage leaf) and top with shallots, peanuts, and extra red chili if desired.
6. Serve and savor it.

3.8 Asian Vegan Red Tofu with Curry Sauce

There are plenty of vegetables in this Thai red curry tofu, which comes together fast and tastes like a milder version of your beloved takeout meal.

Time taken: 55 minutes

Servings: Two persons

Ingredients:

- One packet of tofu (firm, drained, and chopped)
- Half cup of Coconut milk
- Two bell peppers
- Two tablespoons of Peanut butter

For Red curry paste:

- Two teaspoons of coriander seeds
- One teaspoon of cumin
- Red chili and salt as per your taste
- Four teaspoons of Fresh lemongrass
- One teaspoon of lime leaf
- Three teaspoons of Garlic
- One tablespoon of oil

Instructions:

1. To make a smooth paste, combine all of the ingredients mentioned under "for red curry paste."
2. This paste just takes a few minutes to produce, but it can last for days if sealed in an airtight container of olive oil.
3. Squeeze in some lime juice and season with salt and pepper. Mix it all.
4. Cut the tofu into slices and press with a paper towel. For a few seconds, click the button once more. There is a significant amount of water in there.
5. Heat oil in a pot over a low flame. Add the chili flakes and fried the tofu and capsicum for five minutes before tossing and frying the other side of the tofu for another five minutes.
6. Add salt, pepper, and soy sauce to taste. Remove the mixture from the pan. Set it aside for now.
7. Toss in the tofu, capsicum, and peanuts. Continue to cook for another 5-10 minutes.
8. If you think the sauce is thick for your liking.
9. You can also add spoons of water and mix it well until the consistency becomes as per your liking.
10. Serve with rice and pasta as a side dish.

3.9 Asian Vegan Banh Gio

Bánh gio is a steamed street snack that originated in Northern Vietnam. It is a thin, savory snack that is perfect any time of day, made with a rice flour outer sheet, pork, mushroom, and onion filling, and a banana leaf wrapper that gives it a distinctive fragrance. But in this recipe, we will not use pork or beef, but we will use tofu.

Time taken: 55 minutes

Servings: Four persons

Ingredients:

For Wrappers:

- One pound banana leaves, frozen

For Flour Mixture:

- One and Half cups starch. It should be corn.
- Three tablespoons of potato starch
- Three cans of vegetable broth
- Oil
- Half cup rice flour
- Salt and pepper as per your taste
- Four cups water

For Filling:

- One medium onion

- Two tablespoon cooking oil
- One pound tofu
- Two teaspoons sugar
- Pepper and salt as per your taste

Instructions:

1. Clean and wash banana leave. Cut out foil wrap pieces that are the same size as the finished pyramids.
2. In a big nonstick kettle, combine all of the ingredients.
3. Boil it over medium to high heat. The mixture should thicken after some time. It should be dense enough to prevent the filling from falling in but small enough to cover the wrappers' corners quickly. Remove the pan from the heat.
4. Take a food processor. Chop onions and mushrooms in it separately.
5. Heat oil in a wok over medium flame.
6. Add onion and tofu in a wok and cook it for five minutes or until it is light brown and fragrant.
7. Season with more spices if desired.
8. Place one sheet of foil on top of banana leave. Begin creating the first folds to shape the pyramid's first point.

9. Fill it with a spoon of rice flour mixture in it.
10. Fill the middle with the filling mixture made before. Encase the filling with a spoonful of the rice flour mixture.
11. Cover it completely.
12. Take a large wok and boil water in it.
13. Let it simmer over high temperature. Fill the steamer rack with all of the banh gio. The cooking time is about 55 minutes or less.
14. Serve it when ready. You can also garnish it.

3.10 Asian Vegan Corn Congee

In Asian nations, congee is a sort of rice porridge or gruel. The term "congee" is derived from the Tamil word "kanji." When served as plain rice congee, it is often accompanied by side dishes. Congee is often eaten as a meal on its own when other foods like meat, fish, and seasonings are added during the preparation process, particularly for persons who are unwell. Congee has as many names as there are ways to make it. Despite its various varieties, it is normally a thick rice porridge that has mostly decomposed after being cooked in water for a long time.

Time taken: One hour

Servings: three persons

Ingredients:
- One cup rice, uncooked
- Seven c. vegetable broth
- One fresh corn ear
- One piece of fresh ginger
- Salt and pepper as per your taste

For the Topping:
- Three sliced spring onions
- Half cup peanuts
- Six tablespoons sesame oil, roasted
- Sesame seeds, three tablespoons

- Three tablespoons chile sauce

Instructions:

1. Rinse rice until the water runs clear under cold running water. In a multi-functional pressure cooker, combine the rice with 6 cups of vegetable broth.
2. Remove the corn kernels off the cob and split them into three pieces.
3. In a saucepan with rice and broth, combine the kernels, cob bits, and ginger. Close the lid and secure it.
4. Set the timer for 30 minutes and choose the Porridge option. Allow for a 10- to a 15-minute build-up of pressure.
5. Allow 15 minutes to remove pressure using the natural-release technique, as directed by the manufacturer.
6. Remove the lid by unlocking it. Check the congee's consistency. If you prefer a thinner congee, add one tablespoon of broth at a time until the desired consistency is attained.
7. Remove the corn cob pieces and season generously with salt and white pepper.
8. Congee should be divided into bowls. Evenly sprinkle the toppings.

Note: I have used a pressure cooker in this recipe. You can use anything such as pan or wok.

Chapter 4: Most Famous Asian Vegetarian Wok Recipes

A vegetarian meal made with spices and flavors from Asian nations is known as Asian vegetarian food. Vegetables, fresh fruit, dried fruit, legumes, dairy products, tofu, cereal, grains, and vegetarian gelatin are common ingredients. It is ideal for vegetarians who want a vegetarian dinner since it contains no meat, fish, or eggs.

The greatest thing about Asian food is how vegetarian-friendly it is. Some of the greatest Asian vegetarian dishes are among the greatest Asian dishes. The second great aspect is that the delectable meals appear to go on forever. Here are some of the finest vegetarian Asian recipes available online that you may prepare at home.

4.1 Asian Vegetarian Wok Spicy Garlic Edamame

Edamame is the Japanese word for juvenile soybean, derived from the terms "stem" and "bean." Edamame is a healthy food that is high in minerals and protein. Edamame, or whole, unprocessed organic soybeans, may be part of a nutritious diet. While plain or mildly salted edamame is a wonderful on-the-go snack, the spicy variation below is one of my all-time favorites. This recipe for spicy garlic edamame is simple, nutritious, and tasty. It is also simple to make and enjoyable to consume. Plus, edamame is a great source of vegan protein.

In fact, some research suggests that whole, raw soy is one of the world's healthiest foods. Many of the studies that show soy is harmful to your health were conducted on highly processed soy. For the healthiest soy consumption, stick to organic whole edamame that has not been processed. Edamame has a high protein, fiber, and excellent carbohydrate content and vitamins and minerals, including calcium, vitamin K, vitamin C, and folate. It also has the ability to lower cholesterol levels.

Time taken: 55 minutes

Servings: three persons

> **Ingredients:**
> - Salt and pepper as per your taste
> - Half teaspoon orange zest

- One tablespoon of roasted sesame seeds.
- Half cup veggie broth
- One tablespoon honey
- Two tablespoon of vegetable oil
- Soy sauce, half cup
- Four garlic cloves, chopped.
- One teaspoon of ginger, grated
- Five cup edamame

Instructions:

1. Mix liquid ingredients and spices together in a bowl.
2. Let it boil over medium flame.
3. Boil it until it becomes thick and half of the mixture has been dried.
4. Heat a wok over a moderate flame in the meanwhile.
5. Add oil and all other remaining ingredients in it.
6. Let it cook for a while.
7. Mix the above-prepared mixture in a sauce.
8. Let it simmer for five minutes.
9. Your dish is prepared. Serve with any garnishing.

4.2 Asian Vegetarian Wok Veggie with Peanut Butter Sauce

Vegetable Stir Fry with Peanut Sauce is a delicious main meal that takes less than 30 minutes to prepare. You may simply change up the vegetables to suit your preferences. Any of the veggies in this dish may be replaced with ones that you like. This dinner comes together in a flash. Chopping up all of the veggies takes the most time. It took about 10 minutes to prepare the actual meal. Prepare your rice, noodles, or anything else you are serving with this veggie stir fry ahead of time.

Time taken: Thirty minutes

Servings: Four persons

Ingredients:

For the Sauce:
- Peanut butter, two tablespoons
- Two tablespoons soy sauce
- Two tablespoons of chile sauce
- Half cup of water
- One tablespoon of maple syrup

For the Stir-fry:
- One tablespoon of oil
- One garlic clove
- One ginger root
- One onion

- Three cups fresh or frozen veggies
- One pound of snow peas
- A handful of corns
- Three and a half oz. glass noodles

Instructions:

1. Defrost the frozen vegetables.
2. Chop all vegetables.
3. Put the peanut butter, soy sauce, sweet chili sauce, water, and syrup in a large mixing basin. Mix everything together with a spoon until it is a lovely, creamy sauce. Lemongrass may be used if desired.
4. Cook the noodles. Drain and rinse under cold water when done.
5. Heat the oil in a wok. Pour the garlic, ginger, onion, sugar snaps, and baby corn in it.
6. Add vegetables in it. Saute them.
7. Reduce the heat to medium-low and stir in the sauce and noodles.
8. Allow for another 3-5 minutes of simmering.

4.3 Asian Vegetarian Wok Korean Bok Choy

For some individuals, particularly those who grew up in a traditional Cantonese household, this bok choy stir fry may seem too basic. However, recreating this famous Chinese meal at home to taste like those served in restaurants is surprisingly difficult. Bok choy is just as popular as Chinese broccoli and choy sum, and it is just as simple to prepare.

Bok choy leaves are crisp and somewhat bitter, with a faint grassy flavor. The stems are either white or light green in color. The texture is crisp, with a wonderful crunch that reminds me of celery. Bok choy has a mild, neutral flavor and may be prepared in a variety of ways with a variety of spices.

Time taken: One hour

Servings: Four persons

Ingredients:
- Two bunches broccoli
- A third of a cup of oyster sauce
- Two tablespoons of soy sauce
- Half teaspoon white sugar
- Oil
- Three garlic cloves
- One red chili
- Four bok choy bunches

Instructions:

1. Cut each bunch of Chinese broccoli in half to remove the stems from the leaves. Set aside the leaves.
2. Combine the oyster sauce, soy sauce, and white sugar in a small bowl.
3. In a wok, heat the vegetable oil over high heat. Stir-fry for approximately 30 seconds after adding the garlic and chili. Stir in the Chinese broccoli stems for approximately two minutes. Toss in the wok.
4. Chinese broccoli leaves, bok choy, and a variety of oyster sauces Stir-fry for another two minutes, or until the greens have wilted somewhat.
5. Take the wok off the heat and serve.

4.4 Asian Vegetarian Wok Di San Xian

Di San Xian is a trademark of northern Chinese cuisine. Di San Xian translates to "three jewels from the earth," referring to the dish's potato, eggplant, and green pepper. These are the most frequent veggies in any northern Chinese market, and they are available all year.

Like many other Northeast Chinese cuisines, the cuisine stresses a family style presented in a rustic, sometimes seen as less sophisticated manner. On the other hand, the cooking technique transforms these three ordinary veggies into a feast that makes your mouth wet just by looking at them.

Time taken: 55 minutes

Servings: Four persons

Ingredients:
- Two eggplants, long
- Half cup cornstarch
- One pound potatoes, thickly sliced
- One green pepper, peeled and chopped into tiny chunks.
- One chopped green onion
- Two chopped garlic cloves
- For frying, oil

Sauce:

- Two tablespoon of soy sauce
- Half teaspoon of sugar
- Salt and pepper as per your taste
- A half tbsp. soy sauce (dark)
- One tablespoon cornstarch
- Three tablespoons of water

Instructions:

1. Soak the eggplants in gently salted water for twenty minutes.
2. Drain and apply a thin coating of cornstarch to the surface.
3. Combine all of the stir-frying sauce ingredients in a small bowl.
4. Heat the oil in the wok to create a 3 cm oil layer.
5. Place the potatoes in the pan and heat until they are fully done.
6. Place eggplant and cook it gently until it is completely done.
7. Green pepper should be fried for 10 seconds.
8. Green onion and garlic should be fried till fragrant.
9. Pour in the stir fry sauce. Let it boil.
10. Combine all the remaining ingredients. Fry until all of the pieces are evenly coated.
11. Serve with steaming rice.

4.5 Asian Vegetarian Wok Teriyaki Cauliflower and Kale

If you enjoy teriyaki, you should try this flavorful recipe. By utilizing cauliflower as the meaty highlight, I have given chicken teriyaki a vegan makeover. This delicious teriyaki cauliflower is full of plant-based deliciousness yet has no added sugar. This recipe is a great mixture of vegetables. It is easy to make as well.

Time taken: One hour

Servings: Four persons

Ingredients:
- Half cup juice, that should be pineapple
- One and half tablespoons tamari
- One tablespoon sesame oil, unrefined
- Two big garlic cloves
- One chili pepper
- One teaspoons ginger root
- One tablespoon avocado oil
- One pound florets of cauliflower
- One package baby kale
- Two tablespoons sesame seeds, roasted
- Salt and pepper as per your taste

Instructions:

1. Mix together all the spices and liquid ingredients in a bowl.
2. Take a wok and heat oil in it. Cook vegetables in it, while occasionally stirring, until the cauliflower is nicely browned.
3. Add seasonings as per your taste.
4. Add the prepared mixture and all other remaining ingredients.
5. Serve with any garnishing.

4.6 Asian Vegetarian Madras Curry

Curry is basically based on Thai or Indian cuisine. Curry has a quite variety in its flavors and recipes. I have written Madras curry, which is vegetarian. It can be served with rice. You will get its ingredients from Asian market. I have not mentioned quantity of each ingredient here because it varies a lot. You can add ingredients according to your taste. Let's get started.

Time taken: two hours

Servings: Four persons

Ingredients:
- Ghee
- Onion
- Coriander

- Garlic
- Clean ginger
- Salt and chili as per your taste
- Citrus zest
- Finely sliced tomatoes
- Curry Powder
- Coconut milk

Instructions:

1. Heat oil in a wok. Add the sliced onion, chopped garlic, and smashed ginger to the oil. Stir for 10 minutes until the onions become very tender.
2. Add curry powder, salt, and chili powder. Mix and cook it all for some time until it becomes aromatic.
3. Boost the flame to normal, and add the coconut milk and tomatoes in it. Cook it for some time.
4. In order to finish the sauce, add chopped coriander to it.
5. Just before eating, sprinkle the lemon zest for garnishing.

4.7 Asian Vegetarian Spinach and Potatoes with Tofu Kofta

This recipe is a modern version of Traditional Indian recipe. I have added tofu instead of meat in it. It has all nutrients and fiber in it. That will be quite healthy for humans. This flavorful and delicious recipe can be served with white rice.

Time taken: One hour

Servings: Four persons

Ingredients:

- one onion
- one garlic
- two small-medium potatoes
- Half pile of coriander
- Half teaspoon cumin
- Half teaspoon turmeric
- Half teaspoon mustard
- One pot of vegetable reserve or broth
- 300 g of tofu, chopped and firm
- Coconut Milk as per your need
- ½ teaspoon of lemon zest
- Water

Instructions:

1. Chop all the vegetables.
2. Heat oil in a wok. Add the garlic and onion in it and cook for 5 mins or until it becomes tender. Keep half of this substance out and put it away in a tray.
3. Put the rest onion in the frying pan with the cumin, turmeric, and mustard and mix and cook it for 3 minutes.
4. Add the potato cubes and water as per your need and half a pot of vegetable supply. Mix it so that it will dissolve. Cover with a lid, switch the heat to low and boil for around 15-20 mins.
5. Meanwhile, place the tofu in a bowl and mix with salt as per your taste, a decent black pepper, and grind.
6. Form the mixture of tofu into four small balls per individual. In a frying pan, heat oil on moderate flame and fry until golden brown everywhere.
7. Remove the Tofu koftas from the pan.
8. Put the koftas in a boiling mixture and boil gently.
9. Add the spinach, then remove the pan from the flame, place the lid on, and keep it on the side for 10 minutes. Mix it in the spinach. Put over a little lemon zest and stir it straight. Serve it.

4.8 Asian Vegetarian Veggie Butter Curry

Butter curry is Thai-based cuisine. It is quite famous among its natives and worldwide. It is very flavorful and delicious because of its spices. You can easily get these spices from an Asian shop.

Time taken: Two hours

Servings: Four persons

Ingredients:
- Two tablespoons of butter
- One huge white onion, tiny dice
- Two big garlic cloves
- One teaspoon clean ginger
- One tablespoon Garam Masala
- One tablespoon curry powder
- One tablespoon cilantro powder
- Half teaspoon paprika
- A quarter tablespoon cinnamon
- Chili flakes about quarter tablespoon
- Two tomatoes
- One 400 ml coconut milk bottle

Instructions:

1. Heat coconut oil or butter in a wide skillet or pot over moderate-low heat until it is melted. Add the onion in it and cook for around 6 minutes or until it is translucent.
2. Garlic and ginger are added and sautéed for 5 minutes until it turns out to be aromatic, then add garam masala, curry powder, cilantro, paprika, and cinnamon. Let it cook for around 1 minute, thus swirling periodically.
3. Add the chili flakes and tomatoes to the jar. For around 15 minutes, let all the sauce boil until the sauce thickness increases, and it will become a strong and dark red-brown shade.
4. Remove it from flame and put it into a mixer, and add salt as per your taste. Then add up to a quarter a cup of water in it if the mixture is too heavy to incorporate. Blend in batches if you have a small blender.
5. Put the sauce back into the tub. Add coconut milk and sugar to it. You would insert your cooked lentils, tomatoes, chickpeas, and vegan chicken at this stage and cook it for 10-15 minutes.
6. Represent it with corn and coriander

4.9 Asian Vegetarian Wok Spinach Ravioli

This spinach ravioli dish is perfect comfort food, with a beautiful, creamy tomato basil sauce that will have you begging for more. You will start with cheese-filled ravioli and cover them with a creamy, cheesy sauce flavored with garlic, basil, and tomato.

Time taken: 55 minutes

Servings: Four persons

Ingredients:
- Tomato Sauce (three cups)
- One teaspoon oil
- One minced garlic clove
- One mug mozzarella cheese, shredded
- Half cup shredded Cottage cheese
- Half cup milk
- Half teaspoon oregano, dry
- Half teaspoon nutmeg powder
- A quarter teaspoon of pepper
- One container of chopped spinach
- Wrappers for 36 tons of won
- One beat egg white

Instructions:

1. Tomato Sauce should be made ahead of time and kept warm.
2. Heat the oil over medium-high heat in a wok. Sauté for 1 minute after adding the garlic.
3. In a food processor, add the garlic, mozzarella cheese, and the following ingredients mentioned above. Mix it well.
4. Spoon approximately one tablespoon spinach mixture into the middle of each won ton wrapper, working with one wrapper at a time.
5. Apply egg white to the wrapper's edges and pull two opposing corners together.
6. To seal the edges, use a fork to press them together to create a triangle. Using the remaining won ton wrappers, spinach mixture, and egg white, repeat the process.
7. Boil water in a wok. Cook for 2 minutes, stirring once.
8. With a slotted spoon, remove ravioli from water. Put aside and keep warm. Carry on with the rest of the ravioli.
9. Fill shallow dishes halfway with ravioli and top with sauce.

4.10 Asian Vegetarian Spicy Pasta

This pasta meal is spicy, but it can also be made quickly. And most importantly, it is quite simple to make. You can also make any variations as you like. This is a spicy recipe. If you do not like to eat such spicy food then, simply omit the chilies from the recipe for a milder taste.

Time taken: 55 minutes

Servings: Four persons

Ingredients:

- One cup of pasta to pick as per your liking
- One tablespoon of olive oil
- One teaspoon of seed cumin
- Three sliced garlic cloves
- One tiny sliced onion
- Three thin, diced tomatoes
- One tablespoon powder of turmeric
- One teaspoon of option curry powder
- One tablespoon powder of coriander
- Ground red chili as per your taste

- Salt as per your taste
- One cup of water or, as needed

Instructions:

1. Heat oil in a wok. Let it get warm.
2. Add garlic, onions, and cumin seed and cook for a while.
3. Add the tomatoes and cook them until they are tender. Include all the dried spices and salt.
4. Fry for one or two minutes.
5. Add pasta and water. Mix properly, then turn off stir fry mode.
6. Cover it with a lid and let it cook for twenty minutes.
7. Serve it as per your liking.

Conclusion

Asian Vegetarian food is one of the easiest comfort food that you can prepare at home. Asian Vegetarian foods come in different varieties. After reading this book, you will realize that making your favorite Asian food at home is not difficult at all. In this book, we discussed in detail the history and origin of Asian Vegetarian Wok Food. This cookbook includes 50 recipes that contain green tofu recipes, plant-based recipes, vegan recipes, and famous vegetarian recipes. You can easily make these recipes at home without the supervision of any kind. So, start cooking today and enjoy cooking your delicious Asian foods at home.

Printed in Great Britain
by Amazon